Empowerment Through Forgiveness

Opening The Gate of The Soul

Forgiveness is a smile!

Henry Petru

Expanded Edition

Empowerment Through Forgiveness

Opening The Gate of The Soul

Henry Petru

Published By
Positive Imaging, LLC
bill@positive-imaging.com

ISBN   9781944071431

Cover by Henry Petru

The emblem on the cover alludes to the opening of the human soul to forgiveness. The triangle represents the Triune God-Spirit. The swirl represents Divine Universal Consciousness embracing and piercing the Divine Heart-Soul. This opens the human heart-gate and floods the Heart-Soul with Divine Love, Awareness and Compassion.

Preface

Every answer has a question. If we don't have an answer, there is no question. The answer presented here is: We can change the world. The question is: Can we change the world? A follow-up question is: How?

When we know—really, absolutely know—that we have the power to change the world, we also will know that we have the compassion to accept the world as it is in the present moment. In that consciousness, if we do want to change anything, we must transform within ourselves the change we want, and do it in the unwavering belief that the transformation will be reflected throughout the planet as a shift in the resonant world hologram .

What does that mean? A hologram is a representation that contains all the possibilities impressed upon it. If it is divided up or broken apart into many pieces, each piece contains a complete duplicate of the original whole. Metaphorically, all creation exists as a hologram, containing all possibilities that Creation has imbedded therein. But, in our personal life, our belief in separation from ourselves, each other and our Creator has shattered the hologram into many fragments. Each fragment, each individual human, however, contains and reflects completely the original whole. We have within us all the potential and all the possibilities that could ever be. A change in one piece, one life, affects all life; changing something in ourselves is reproduced as a change throughout the world hologram. That is our potential through the power of oneness.

How do we create harmony out of this chaos, this shattered hologram? We have an answer. One of the greatest empowerments of change is forgiveness. When we forgive, we open the gate of our soul and allow the beasts that torment our heart and the pain that grates our spirit to escape. Through this gate we release and let go our misery. Conversely, through this gate we also receive and accept the empowerment of the peace that forgiveness bestows.

How do we arrive at this peace, this forgiveness? You have in your hands the answer. This book lays out the plan, and the steps, of the Forgiveness Process that opens the gate of the soul. After practicing the steps of the Forgiveness Process, you come to understand that forgiveness is the answer and that opening the gate of the soul through forgiveness is the question. The answer opens the gate of the soul and releases our obsessions with things of form.

Contents

Dedication

This book is dedicated to
all who awaken
to the return of feeling good

Acknowledgements

This book began as a chapter in another book I was writing but it became so powerful to me and presented such potential for good that I broke it out as a book in its own right. In gratitude, I acknowledge and give thanks first to Divine Source for inspiration and intuitive insight and instruction. I am most grateful to Frances Meiser for guidance, loving encouragement and unwavering support. I give special thanks and gratitude to Susan Jaeschke (Jazz) and Jane Demars for editorial work, direction, advice and encouragement. I am very grateful to all who inspire me and stimulate my thinking. Finally, I acknowledge and give thanks to and for my wonderful body–my home on Earth. Every day, I am grateful to Life for life.

Introduction

There is no greater power
Than that of an idea
Whose time has come.

Victor Hugo

Life is feelings, preferably good and happy feelings. Forgiveness is the dissolution of feelings and thoughts about reactions we have to events or incidents, especially those that are hurtful or that evoke negative emotions. The Forgiveness Process presented in this book culminates in love of self, and love of Self, and when you love your Self, you love everything.

The Forgiveness Process can be applied to any situation, any injury perceived or real, any injustice, any argument or disagreement, any hurtful incident. It is effective individually as well as in a group, with the group's consensus. With understanding and consensus, it could even be effective among nations in resolving differences. There are many benefits to forgiving. Some of these are:

- A healthy self image
- Not being upset by others' behavior
- The ability to detach from the negative
- Love of self and others
- A joyful life
- Being grateful and living gratitude
- Inner peace
- Being in the moment

Chapter one provides insight into the spiritual and biological/neurological reasons for why forgiveness works. It covers who we are, the purpose of our body, and the oneness of life. An interesting analogy comparing life to a stack of CDs is presented. Also referenced are scientific studies describing activity within the brain when forgiveness takes place.

Chapter two postulates that forgiveness is more than a choice, that there is a spiritual and neurological need to forgive. Further expansion of the oneness principle is presented together with how our own perceptions distort what we see. This chapter presents a good background for understanding the Forgiveness Process.

Chapter three shows how we begin to forgive with gratitude. Being grateful is the first element of manifestation, the expression or coming into evidence of that which we request or desire. We find that if gratitude is not present in the Forgiveness Process, the forgiving itself is incomplete and nothing changes.

The fourth chapter delves into the core of the Forgiveness Process. In it, we learn how forgiveness is individual and personal and how we cannot directly forgive another person. The chapter presents three steps of action and reaction and the four levels within our selves that must be reached to dissolve whatever we wish to forgive. All true forgiveness contains these elements, even if we are not conscious of them.

In chapter five and six, we expose obstacles to forgiveness and suggest ways to dissolve them with compassion and love.

Chapter seven demonstrates surrender and release as experiences which take place within ourselves. These experiences demand that we reach for our Higher Self and release whatever is riveting us to a way of life we may not want. The chapter covers major steps in further understanding, and helping with, the process by which forgiveness takes place. We also learn about the bathroom sanctuary techniques that strengthen and empower forgiving.

Chapter eight considers ideas about the present moment, the instant of all reality. We learn that we cannot forgive in the past or the future, and this chapter expands the idea that forgiving, as all of life, can take place only in the present moment.

Chapter nine presents some rewards of forgiveness. It contains a bit of metaphysics and spirituality with a practical nuance.

When absorbed and understood, Empowerment Through Forgiveness will enhance your life and bestow the benefits already listed, and more. I urge the reader to learn to forgive consciously and often.

1

Why Forgiveness Works
Life is like playing a stack of CDs

Asking why forgiveness works is like asking why the wind blows. There are explanations for why the wind blows, and there are reasons why forgiveness works.

As for the wind, looking into meteorology and weather, we find forces that power and move the air, resulting in what we call wind or breeze. Our findings reveal phenomena such as low and high atmospheric pressure, cold and warm fronts, the jet stream; we find hurricanes, typhoons, cyclones and tornadoes. Then we find that there are other forces that contribute, like the power of the sun and the gravitational pull of the moon. So, there could be quite a discussion if a meteorologist or scientist were to explain all this.

Explaining what makes forgiveness work may be even more challenging. Basically, forgiveness works when and because we forgive ourselves; because our life is personal and takes place totally within us. Therefore, the need to forgive is generated within, as is forgiveness itself. Later in this book, we will learn how to forgive by applying steps of the Forgiveness Process. But why is the Forgiveness Process effective? What makes forgiveness work? There seem to be both spiritual and biological/ neurological explanations.

Spiritual Explanation

In order to forgive, we must have been hurt or offended by someone or something. The offending or hurting is an internal process, as is the forgiving, that restores the Self and works with attitudes such as surrender, gratitude and acceptance. When these attributes interplay in the Forgiveness Process, we feel better about ourselves. We feel peaceful because peace comes when we have nothing to forgive, when we have worked through our hurts and have forgiven ourselves for the way we responded to these hurts. In peace, we understand the effects these hurts had on our lives, and the feelings generated by forgiving are more than benefits. They are life-generating rewards.

Spiritually, forgiveness works because of the principle of oneness. The phrase 'I forgive you" lacks meaning because there is no you. There is not even us. There is only oneness. Life takes place totally and completely within this oneness. Our body is merely solidified energy in form, not the essential existence of who we are. The body is not a who; it is a what. According to the principle of oneness, everything in the universe is made of the same energy/ substance and is shaped into an infinite number of forms, and when we humans look at each other, that energy appears as the solidified three-dimensional form of the human body. The absolute only purpose for our body is to give the God-part we call our soul an experience of life on earth, to give us a form through which the life essence itself can experience the physical level. Our soul can, and probably has, experienced life in other body forms and on other planets.

All humans are the same in everything except the external appearance of the body where we all look different, each with different features. But in these features, we're also all the same. We all have a mouth, a nose, eyes, etc. Inside the body, we're even more identical. We all have a heart located in the same place, a liver located in the same place, etc, and they all look pretty much alike. All of our organs inside the body are identical and in the same location in each one of us. By way of a metaphor, the human race is like an ant colony or a bee hive, where one unit–the ant colony or the bee hive–exhibits one common consciousness, one form, but appears as multiple physicalities in an all-encompassing oneness.

Oneness encompasses our life-essence, our spirit or soul, which also is the same in all of us. Nay, it is more than the same. It is the One Energy Mass from which we project. It's called by many names: God, Higher Power, Spirit, The Universe, among others. In this One Energy Mass, we're as united as are boundless drops of water (the Spirits/Souls) in the same Eternal Ocean. Our bodies, like grains of sand inside every drop, appear as individuals. But the engulfing drops of water representing our spirits/souls are united in the ocean, boundless and indistinguishable. Therefore, during the Forgiveness Process, in forgiving ourselves, all the grains of sand (everyone, as indistinguishable drops in the One Ocean) are forgiven. These include those we may like or dislike, since we're all one, all of the same vibration. In this way, we ameliorate any guilt we may feel toward others (the other grains of sand), including anyone we perceive as having done us harm.

Since the grain of sand, our body, inside the drop of water, the essence of our being, is like our body inside our spirit/soul, we can see how our physical life takes place inside us, inside the drop, within the spirit that we are, and not in the world around us. By example, suppose you meet a friend you haven't seen in a long time. Why are you happy to see your friend? Is it because you and your friend were separate? No! It is because, through the principle of oneness, your friend awakens in you that part of yourself that projects out into the visible form and manifests as your friend. Your friend is you! Every reaction to every event that comes into our life is our life, and it is directly related to and proportional to the intensity of our perception of these events. To understand this better, let's examine a metaphor. Later in this book, in the chapter about the present moment, we will learn that, on some level, everything is already created and all possibilities exist simultaneously, right now. We radiate a vibration according to our state of consciousness and whatever resonates with that vibration in the realm of all possibilities is what is drawn to us, and may show up in our life. This leads us to a picture of life as a stack of CDs (many life planes, many possibilities, many states of consciousness) that stand ready to be played. Everyone, all the grains of sand, has his/her own stack of CDs. Together, all these stacks are the collective consciousness of the human race. Our individual life, our reality, in any moment is the CD we're playing. Other realities exist simultaneously on the other CDs (other life planes) either higher or lower than the one we're playing. Unless we eject the one we're playing now through surrender and insert another one through choice and acceptance, preferably one higher, we will stay where we are, constantly replaying our life over and over. We will be on automatic replay, and we will be in a rut. Through forgiving ourselves that in which we are stuck, we can get out of that rut.

Continuing with the metaphor of the CDs, choosing a higher level CD, a higher consciousness, advances our life just as choosing a lower

CD backs us away from the progress we've already made. Our stack of CDs exists in our world, in our reality, and does not cross over to anyone else's stack, although the totality of all the CD stacks constitutes the collective consciousness of oneness.

The forgiveness CD exists on a high level. When we choose to forgive, we tune in and mesh with the vibrations of that reality and leave behind the reality where the offense took place. We cannot live on both levels. We surrender judgement and allow entry into our life that with which we are in sync, in tune; that which matches our vibration and we move from a negative feeling to peace.

In the oneness of all, we are not individuals in our forgiveness. Neither are we alone in our joy and sorrow. When we feel joy or sorrow, we are in sync with the vibrations of collective consciousness, the oneness, in these areas. On a certain level of the collective consciousness of this oneness, joy or sorrow are present according to the values that we hold for ourselves. This is true of all other emotions and feelings as well, including forgiveness. Therefore, we can conclude that forgiveness works because there is a level of collective consciousness, a oneness CD, where it exists. Practicing the Forgiveness Exercise, which appears later in this book, lifts us to this level, and we tune in. When forgiveness is complete, we enjoy the peace and serenity offered by the Oneness of the Eternal Ocean.

Biological/Neurological Explanation

In the brain, there are neurological, chemical and electrical actions, reactions and paths that process the decisions, emotions and feelings associated with all our perceptions of life events. Hence, these processes interplay with our concept of forgiveness.

Scientific studies by A.J. Clark at the University of Arizona, Molecular and Biological Division, have shown that the healing power of forgiveness is a process that takes place in the brain. A.J. Clark describes it as follows:

1. The fear center in the brain (the amygdala) is triggered by a hurtful memory.
2. This memory-triggered fear activates anger.
3. Under certain stimulation (like the desire to forgive - my insert), the frontal cortex of the brain interrupts the process and calms the fear response in the amygdala.
4. Tension and muscles relax, signaling the cortex that forgiveness has occurred, interrupting the path from the rhinal cortex to the amygdala.
5. Further attempts to bring on anger show that the memories no longer stimulate the amygdala. Thus, no further stress or anger occurs, and the forgiveness is neurologically complete.

Listings of scientific studies about the healing power of forgiveness can be found on the government web site: www.ncbi.nlm.nih.gov

This study is very significant because the plasticity of the brain allows everyone the ability to learn to forgive themselves, no matter how hardened the character or how old the body. This is good news to be carried to every correctional institute in the country. This is a way to peaceful living even if an individual does not favor the spiritual explanation of why or how forgiveness works. Forgiving is multifaceted. Yet, it is a simple act. Even though the steps outlined in the Forgiveness Process seem to be individual acts, they are facets of the one act of forgiving. In the next chapter, we will explore why we feel the need to forgive.

2

Why We Need To Forgive
It's more than a choice

The psychology of need was developed by Abraham Maslow in the 1940s. He established a pyramid of need ranging from the basic, such as food and shelter, to self-actualization, such as creativity, ability and expression.

So, what is a need? Not a want, which is a preference, but a true need, which is an essential to life. Having a need for something connotes a lack of something. If we are lacking, we are incomplete in the area of lack. Something is missing. By analogy, if my car is out of gas, I could say: "My car doesn't have its need met". The car has a lack. It is perfect as an object of creation, but incomplete in the purpose for which it was created as long as it has an empty gas tank. In like manner, we are incomplete when we diminish our life and cannot complete our purpose.

Everything is perfect unto its creation. We, however, through wrongful thinking, lifestyle and choice, punch holes in the perfection that we are. We drain our life force, our energy, and produce a vacuum in our wellbeing, a lack that causes us to feel the need to forgive. Filling this need to forgive and to reconcile dissolves this vacuum, this lack. We now have a choice: live the status quo, fragmented by needs, or reconcile with ourselves, forgive ourselves and, thereby, reconcile with others by means of that part of forgiveness called exoneration. Through forgiveness, we reconnect with ourselves and heal a separation caused by fear of judgement. If we feel that there is a problem, if we feel a separation from our perfection, we can be sure that there is something to be forgiven. To find what that is (the answer), we must live the problem (the question). If something hurts, precipitates fear, causes guilt, or in any way is judged to make us feel uncomfortable, we are living the problem, the question. From this, we can find the answer. Then we know what to forgive.

Looking at Maslow's psychology of need, we can discern a two-fold need to forgive: neurological and spiritual. Let's look at the neurological first. The most devastating emotion we can experience is fear, the basis of anger, worry, hatred and so many other feelings and emotions. Let's examine the emotion of fear and how it is healed through forgiveness. Some fear, of course, is good, such as a fear that triggers the neurological 'fight or flight' response and urges us to take appropriate action in the face of a threat. Faced by a ferocious creature, for example, we would not be concerned with what we are going to wear to a party. On the other hand, if we are faced by a bully, we may take a stand and defend ourselves.

The fear we are considering is one that, if forgiven and released, would improve the quality of life. Once this fear is overcome - forgiven and released - that which we feared will not re-enter out lives and, if it does, we may not recognize it as the original fear. If we do, we will perceive it in a different way and will not be afraid of it. The original fear will be only a memory, for true forgiveness will change our perception of it and we will see it as perfect and harmless. Think of it as looking at things through a lens of fear. If we try to change the fear, we get no-where. But, through forgiveness, we change the lens and thereby perceive the perfection of that which we feared. The point is that what we see is perfection, but what we perceive is our judgement of it. This judgement, this perception, is the crux of the problem and the key to forgiveness.

Let me illustrate this with a personal example. I like to walk for exercise and recreation, and I do so every morning and evening that I can. Walking near water, as by a lake, is especially uplifting to me. But I used to have a dreaded fear of stray dogs, or at least dogs not on a leash or without their owners nearby. This fear probably originated on the farm where I grew up and saw rabid dogs. I was taught to have a great fear of dogs with rabies and to avoid them, with explanations of what might result from a bite. This was a good fear, but it carried over into my adulthood as a genuine fear of stray dogs.

One morning, during my walk around my neighborhood, a dog in a yard I was passing charged me very aggressively. It was probably just defending its territory but what I perceived was bared teeth and what I heard was vicious growling. I now know that I attracted this incident to myself because the vibration of my fear resonated with an instinct in the dog, and the dog reacted. I got out of that situation by very slowly backing away and mentally talking to the dog. (Really! Honest!) The point is, my fear resulted from my own perception, my own judgement, of an animal that was created perfect. It was my own doing and the threat I felt was real.

A few weeks later, during my walk again, I encountered two dogs that I judged might threaten me. Again, this was my perception, but it felt real. In this situation, I chose to continue walking without looking at the dogs although, out of the corner of my eye, I saw them circling behind me. It was not easy to continue walking as though nothing was wrong and I expected to hear growls or feel a bite, but nothing happened. After walking a short distance, I looked around to see what the dogs were up to. There were no dogs! Nowhere! They had really been there but must have just gone on their way and paid no attention to me. The lesson, again, was that what I saw was perfection—the dogs were perfect in what they were doing. They were being normal dogs, sniffing around and exploring their world. But my perception of them was my judgement of them. I judged that they were mean and maybe were going to attack me. This judgement, as any judgement, was a limiting belief and forgiving myself would remove this limitation. I do not infer that we, especially children, should not exercise normal caution in the presence of stray animals. I relate these episodes only to show how I healed one of my fears.

These two encounters with dogs that generated intense fear in me were my healings, and they filled my need to forgive myself for feeling this fear and for judging the dogs that were perfect unto their creation. I needed to change the lens of fear and perceive the perfection, the oneness, in which I could forgive myself for creating this fear and reacting to it. Under the principle of oneness, if the dogs had attacked me, they would have been attacking themselves. Recognizing and understanding this interplay of perception and fear opens the gate of the soul and facilitates forgiveness and creates peace.

If we do not forgive, the accumulation of fear in our lives over time may become insurmountable. Fear and other strong emotions contribute to many of our illnesses, and if we harbor destructive emotions within ourselves, some illness may take advantage of our weakened state. The neurological need for forgiveness and letting go is obvious. The psychological benefits also are evident: being stress free and peaceful.

The second need to forgive is spiritual, the need for reconciliation mentioned earlier. It is a cry for oneness, for the realization of who we are. We judge ourselves to be separate from everything: from each other, from the world, from life, even from the source of our creation. If, in being who we are and knowing who we are, either the being or the knowing is absent, we have a belief in separation from the truth. Everything outside the truth of Oneness is a judgement and a fear. The realization of oneness, through forgiving, is the end of fear.

Fear and judgement are great separators, creators of duality. In duality, we must have a reference point against which to pit ourselves, where we perceive that we are not one with the reference point. For example, we cannot know the concept of 'high' unless we reference it to the concept of 'low'. In this way, we perceive everything as opposites, as adversaries, a perception that forces our belief in duality. We even assign duality to the weather when we judge it to be 'bad' or 'good', and use both conditions of good and bad as reference points. In the summer, we complain that it's too hot (as referenced to cold), and in the winter, we complain about the cold (as referenced to hot). So it is in our spiritual life. If we deny a Creator, our reference point, we cannot determine who we are. But if we make the Creator our reference point, all duality dissolves since this reference point is omnipresent Oneness and cannot be compared or referenced against itself. To help us dissolve this belief in duality and restore oneness into our concept, we proceed to the Forgiveness Process, where we release our obsessions with duality.

3

The Power of Gratitude

First comes gratitude. Always! So we begin everything with gratitude. It empowers all that we do, and the Forgiveness Process is no exception. It is fitting that thanksgiving comes first, for giving and receiving happen simultaneously in the present moment where we say in knowing and confidence "thank you" before we ask for anything or make a request. Once we express gratitude, we need only to ask, to make a request, and to open our hearts and arms to receive. The expression "I am grateful" is so powerful that, where we see the absence of gratitude, we also often see evidence of poverty, ill health and much worse. Lack of gratitude, perhaps a form of depression, is a condition in which it is difficult to forgive. There is power in the words "Thank You".

Gratitude enhances performance. We can benefit by getting into the habit of saying "thank you". After all, don't we usually thank someone who does something for us or gives us something? Here's a suggestion: why not thank your Self, and your body? For instance, when you really feel good about something you did, say "thank you' to your Self and to yourself. Thank your body every time it performs well, like after a good workout. Thank your body for all its functions. Thank your mind when you get a good idea, or solve a problem.

Gratitude is a power that enables. Considering that everything possible already exists on some level, thanksgiving is the power that acknowledges this and brings what we ask into existence. So, we begin the process of forgiving with gratitude, in gratitude. Gratitude is a quality, a state of being within. We do not even have to express it; just feel it and be it. Others do not have to know that you are grateful, although their knowing enhances their wellbeing and your relationship with them. But their knowing or not knowing does nothing to the quality or degree of the gratitude because it all happens within us. We set the degree and quality by the degree and quality of our participation. Giving gratitude to elicit recognition or acknowledgement is not true gratitude.

Giving thanks is a benediction, a blessing, indicating an end of something, such as an end to a prayer or a ritual. Most people say "thank you" after they have received, or at the end of a request or event. However, it is expedient that we give thanks in the beginning, before we ask for anything, acknowledging in faith that we have received on some level what we have asked and now await its manifestation. Thus, the benediction, the end of asking, is expressed in faith, as gratitude, in the beginning.

One place we find evidence of the practice of giving thanks before we ask or before an event is in the Bible. There we find a number of occasions when Jesus gave thanks before taking action or performing a miracle. (In the following Biblical quotes, italics are mine.) A prominent example is found in the story of the multiplication of the loaves and fish. "...he took the seven loaves and the fish, and *after giving thanks* he broke them and gave them to the disciples, and the disciples gave them to the crowd" (Luke 15.36). Giving thanks before he fed the crowd may have been the power that allowed the miracle of multiplication. Another notable example is The Last Supper. The Bible states: "Then he took a cup, and *after giving thanks*..." (Luke 22.17). Also, "Then he took a loaf of bread, and *when he gave thanks*, he broke it and gave it to them..." (Luke 22.19). And finally, we find an example from the raising of Lazarus to life: "...and Jesus looked upward and said: 'Father, I thank you for having heard me" (John 11.41). "*When he had said this*, he cried out with a loud voice, 'Lazarus, come out'" (John 11.43). Again, thanksgiving before the act may have been so powerful that it facilitated the miracle, even one of restoring life. (NOTE: Biblical quotes taken from the New Revised Standard Version Bible)

In all things, thanksgiving is an integral "first thought" before we ask, pray, or act. In his book, "The Isaiah Effect", Gregg Braden tells the story about a Native American named David and David's prayer inside a medicine wheel in the desert of New Mexico. The medicine wheel, a circle of stones, is considered to be a sacred place. David went there to pray to end a drought in the area. Gregg gives a touching account of David's action inside the medicine wheel, where gratitude is the principle element. David did not ask, beg or plead for rain but gave thanks for the possibility of the rain as already being present. He understood that the rain already existed on some level and his gratitude was the power that brought it forth.

It may not even be necessary to ask for anything, because gratitude is asking. Saying "thank you" is asking the universe to "thank" you, to reward you, to bless you, and "you" does not even have to be a person. Gratitude, like forgiveness, is love, notably Self love. Unconditional love makes us feel perfect and lovable. You could not ask a blessing, a thank you, on another if you did not harbor love within yourself for your Self. This "thank you", coming from Selflove, binds Infinite Source to you and to everyone else.

Traditionally, gratitude is offered through some form of prayer or ritual. This can be a display with some pageantry or it can be a simple thought with feeling—silent, with no need for words or sounds. To feel gratitude, simply picture or imagine yourself being that for which you are grateful, or imagining already possessing it even as you ask for it. Remember, the asking is integrated into the emotion of gratitude.

For example, you may ask Divine Source for a sunny day because you plan to be outdoors. Give thanks before you ask for the sunny day. In the midst of your expression of gratitude, try to feel yourself 'being the weather' that you want. Use all your senses. Be the light and warmth of the sun; be the cool breeze caressing your face; be the sounds of nature; be the smell of flowers, or freshly mowed grass; be the whisper of wind through the trees; be a tree bending its branches in obedience to the breeze. Be as many aspects as you can imagine of the kind of day you want. As you embody the aspects you want and become them, overflow your heart with gratitude, for you have been blessed with the fulfillment of your request. Then you need do nothing more than be open to receive. This is the essence of David's prayer in the medicine wheel.

Practice saying often the words "I am grateful." While it is wise to choose carefully the words and thoughts that follow the expression "I am" due to the power of this affirmation, nothing will enhance life more and bring more peace and love than being grateful, than feeling and extending honest, sincere gratitude. Thankfulness is like a delicious, refreshing dessert before a sumptuous meal of receiving.

Gratitude is also a form of surrender. To be grateful, one must release some of the emotional attachment to the characteristics of "have" and "mine". For example, you give me a gift and I respond with gratitude. To acknowledge your generosity and express my thankfulness, I surrender, release and give to you my feeling energy expressed as gratitude. It seems like an even trade. Actually, the quality of the exchange of your gift and my gratitude depends on the emotional states of both of us. If the gift is given and received with love, my energy of gratitude could exceed the energy of the gift, or your energy of generosity could exceed the energy of my gratitude. The point is that, in this exchange, we both surrender something. It may even be something to which we are attached, either physically or emotionally.

So, in expressing gratitude, we first give thanks, then surrender attachment in order to realize the manifestation of our request. Giving up attachments may trigger a depressed feeling because of the attachment itself. The act of detaching, however, is a moment of replenishment. In the moment of gratitude, we are filled with grace and awakened and informed that everything is in order and our request is granted. In the act of giving sincere thanks, we live the experience, embodying our emotions, feelings and thoughts. If we do not, our gratitude is only a clanging symbol making beautiful sounds instead of crystallizing the experience. We are gates through which God, our Source, enters this world and, in expressing gratitude, we acknowledge the gates and give thanks and praise to the Source. And we do this before we ask for anything. In the act of forgiving, gratitude is a prerequisite.

4

The Process of Forgiving

From "The Bhagavad Gita" we learn that our relationship with God is love, our relationship with ourselves is forgiveness, and our relationship with each other is acceptance. Love, forgiveness and acceptance—three keys to harmony with God, self and others.

Here, we're concerned with forgiving the relationship with ourselves. To forgive means to dissolve, to release, to let go. You cannot attract forgiveness; it is something you generate within yourself. Thus, you cannot forgive another person. You can only forgive yourself. To forgive another person may be impossible because an offending incident becomes offensive to you only by your reactive feeling toward it. It is not offensive to the perpetrator. For example, an insulting remark is only a remark unless you respond to it. Your own evaluations, judgments and thoughts about your own reactions to the remark are the things to be forgiven. Reactions to events produce emotions that are expressed as feelings. Feelings are more difficult to change or delete than thoughts. Thoughts are processes of conclusion, and form in response to the reactive feelings. The thoughts are at the core of the reaction to the incident and must be the first to be let go in the Forgiveness Process. After you forgive yourself your thoughts, you can change your feelings. For instance, an incident, such as a negative remark directed at you, evokes a reactive feeling in you–perhaps an emotion of resentment. This reactive resentment sparks a thought, a judgment, or an evaluation about how you feel about the reaction itself, rather than how you feel about your reaction to the remark. You probably will feel it in the pit of your stomach. This thought, judgment or evaluation is the underlying issue, the core issue, that must be let go in order for you to forgive yourself and thereby, like a byproduct, also release whoever initiated the offending remark. If you say that you forgive without going to this underlying base issue first, and letting go your evaluation and thoughts about your reaction to the incident, you haven't forgiven anything and your resentment will stay and grow.

Your thoughts about your reaction, the "thoughts behind the feeling", are seated deeply within you and are the core issue associated with every event in your life, good or otherwise, to which you react, because they affect your self-image. An incident-specific core evaluation and thought will always emerge to color every situation to which you respond, whether you act on it or not. This same process works also when you have a good or positive reaction to an event where you feel joy or happiness or love. Obviously, there is nothing to forgive in this case.

This process also applies to forgiving events from the past, memories that hurt. To forgive a past memory, however, you must bring that event into the present moment as though the event had just happened, and follow the steps of the Forgiveness Process outlined later in this chapter. Forgiveness cannot take place in the past because life does not take place in the past, only in the present.

Now the question: How can you do it? How can you go from your reaction to an incident, to thoughts about your reaction to it, to releasing your thoughts about your reaction? Begin by releasing any notion that you primarily need to forgive the other person, for that may not even be possible. Second, invoke the power of intention to change your decision from one of suffering to one of love. Finally, take full responsibility for your reaction to the incident and your thoughts about any hurt or offense you feel. These core issue thoughts must be let go by taking the steps of the Forgiveness Process. **Letting go is accomplished by taking responsibility and releasing the emotional energy of a feeling. You can change this emotional feeling by changing your thoughts.**

By accepting responsibility for your reaction, you become as a shepherd taking charge of the thoughts relating to your reaction. In this capacity, you have the power to accept the thoughts or to let them go. In the practice of forgiveness, the choice must be to let go the thoughts, for if you accept them and hold them, forgiveness cannot occur. The power of your intention to choose love and to let go of the thoughts about your reaction provides the will and determination to exercise your decision, which then brings into your life peace and the potential for a higher level of existence.

To illustrate the process further, let's use the example of someone slapping you. The slap is the incident, an act originating outside of you and being inflicted on you externally. In the Forgiveness Process, most of what follows the slap takes place internally, within you. Remember that everything is neutral until you put a spin on it, until you judge it. Your immediate reaction to being slapped might be, among others, the feeling of anger, hurt, fear, humiliation or resentment. Instantly, or very shortly following your immediate reaction, you have a thought, a judgment, an evaluation about the way you reacted to the incident; that is, your evaluation and thought concerning how you feel not about the slap, but about your feeling about being slapped. It may take some introspection to realize this thought or evaluation. This thought or evaluation is very personal and may show up as disgust, shame, self-rejection, or just not wanting to experience that and it is the base thought that must be healed, must be let go, as the first step in forgiving yourself. This first step may be the hidden meaning of the admonishment "turn the other cheek", a metaphor indicating not an invitation to more abuse, but as a turning inward to let go and release hostile feelings through the process of forgiving yourself your own hostile thoughts. At this point, understand that the one who slapped you has nothing to do with you. It is that person's journey through life, and you need not concern yourself with it. If you do, you may begin to harbor thoughts of revenge and find it very difficult to forgive.

Now let's go to the heart of the Forgiveness Process, to the healing and mending of personal thoughts about your reaction to the incident. This is where we open the gate of the souL First, give gratitude that the possibility of forgiving and healing is present. Then, accepting responsibility, and through the power of intention, detach from the outcome and let go of your thoughts about your reaction to the slap. Through detachment, become the observer of your own process. This requires squelching the "fight" feeling. When the observed looks back at the observer and both unite, there is unity, and joy comes from this awareness whether the observed is God, a game, or a child at play. After you have let go your thoughts about your reaction, release your original reaction to the incident. Then, mentally dissolve the incident itself, the slap, by focusing your attention on something positive and unrelated. In effect, replace one thought with another. This may not be easy, but the reward is great. It is a giant step forward in spiritual growth.

It may be necessary to repeat this Forgiveness Process several times to arrive at complete restoration of peace within you regarding that particular incident. No animosity can exist in your heart after you go through this process and truly feel a closure. If it does, your work is not complete. But if you're at peace after performing the Forgiveness Process Exercise, a memory of the slap may remain but it will not bother you because you will have forgiven yourself and exonerated any feeling toward the person who slapped you.

Forgiving, in general, is not an easy process. Forgiving yourself specifically is even more difficult. There are no bargain days in forgiveness, no 10 or 20 discounts, no holiday sales where forgiving is easier. It takes focus, determination and a strong willingness to do it. You have to "want to", and you can "want to" through the power of intention.

True forgiveness also may induce grieving, since forgiving entails letting go of something very close to you: a thought, feeling and emotion affecting your self-image. In this sense, forgiving is the death of a thought and, as such, may generate grieving. This grief may evolve into a self-image fear issue which can also be dissolved through the Forgiveness Process. The Forgiveness Process is a healing, a getting well. Experiencing the grief heals the grief and allows peace to re-enter your life.

This peace heals your self-image, which is your personal view and opinion of who you are. If your self-esteem is high enough, you may not even have a reaction to a specific incident such as the slap in the foregoing example. This is the realm of higher consciousness. In such a case, there may be nothing to forgive. But if your evaluation of an incident is vulnerable, you become subject to the experience of pain. Thus, in the example above, it is your self-image that causes the anger, hurt, fear, humiliation or resentment that you feel as your reaction to the slap. The slap is the stimulus for your reaction; it is not the cause of it. The cause is your self-image. As we go through the Forgiveness Process on the following pages of this chapter, you will see how this relates to step 3 under The Incident and Reaction.

Underscore the fact that the Forgiveness Process is simple but not easy. You may not be able to forgive yourself the first time you go through it, but it is worth repeating as many times as it takes in order to experience peace. You may choose to say affirmations as you go through the process. That can be helpful because, when your subconscious accepts a sincere affirmation, your heart opens and your affirmation is confirmed and filled.

Going back and examining the episode of the slap, we observe that the Forgiveness Process consists of two components with a total of seven steps. The first component, The Incident and Reaction, is comprised of three steps: (The numbers and letters correspond to the steps referenced and outlined on the following pages.) (1) the incident itself; (2) your reaction to it; (3) your thoughts about and evaluation of your reaction, which is the core issue. The second component, The Forgiving and Healing, is comprised of four steps: (A) giving thanks for the possibility to forgive and heal; (B) taking responsibility and letting go of your thoughts and evaluation about how you reacted; (C) releasing your initial reaction to the incident; (D) dissolving the incident itself. Upon completion of this process, you have cleared the way to attract the joy of grace, tranquility and peace. You also will feel a sense of accomplishment because, as already stated, the process is not easy and will challenge you.

The following chart presents the steps of The Forgiveness Process in an organized and visual manner and may help in understanding the procedure.

The Incident and Reaction
1. The incident
2. Your reaction to it.
3. Your thoughts about and evaluation of your reaction (this is the core issue)

The Forgiving
A. Give gratitude for the possibility of forgiving and healing.
B. Take responsibility and let go of the thoughts about your reaction.
C. Release your actual reaction to the incident.
D. Dissolve the incident by replacing the thought of it with unrelated, positive thoughts.

The Result

Experience grace, tranquility, peace and a sense of accomplishment

We can trace and superimpose these steps on the example of the slap. The following clarification specifically links together, in a simple format, the incident, the reaction, and the forgiving healing.

1. The incident is the slap.
2. Your reaction to it is hurt, anger, fear, humiliation or resentment.
3. Your evaluation and thoughts about your reaction are self-disgust, self shame, self-rejection or not wanting to experience it.

To Forgive:

A. Give thanks
B. Take responsibility for and let go of #3 above
C. Release #2 above
D. Dissolve #1 above

Result: Experience grace, tranquility and peace.

In order to help in thoroughly understanding The Forgiveness Process, consider another example, this one using the weather and your plans for an outdoor activity: a picnic, for instance. (Again, the numbers and letters correspond to the steps above and on the following pages.) The morning of the picnic --- (1) rain! What may be your immediate reaction? (2) Maybe anger at the weather. (3) Instantly, you might think it is stupid or silly to be angry at the weather. You realize that weather is, and weather does. This realization is the evaluation of your reaction, the core issue. To resign yourself to the situation, to forgive yourself, (A) give thanks for the potential to heal. (B) Take responsibility and let go of your thought of stupidity or silliness. (C) Release your reaction toward the rain and dissolve your disappointment about the canceled picnic by realizing that the weather does not check with you concerning your plans. (D) Then, turn your attention to an indoor activity and be at peace with yourself and the weather. Perhaps the rain will play a soft, sizzling sound as background music for whatever activity you choose. This is self-loving forgiveness.

To experience forgiveness in your personal life, do The Forgiveness Exercise on the following page. The exercise personalizes the process, gets you involved and moves you into the heart of forgiveness. For the sake of privacy and to give you more space to write, you may copy and reproduce "The Forgiveness Process Exercise" page only. You may also download and print a copy at:

http://positive-imaging.com/forgiveness.pdf

NOTE: A great help in performing and completing the Forgiveness Process is a practice known as Emotional Freedom Techniques (EFT). This procedure taps on the body energy meridians and brings the body energy into alignment, allowing easy release of emotional blockages to forgiveness. If you have difficulty especially with steps A thru D of the Forgiveness Process, EFT can be a valuable tooL It can restore peace and harmony to your life. For more information on EFT, go to www.emofree.com

The Forgiveness Process Exercise

Use this worksheet to resolve your personal issues. Repeat as necessary. When you feel at peace, you may choose to sign at the bottom of the form as an act of empowerment.

The Incident and Reaction

1. The incident I want to forgive is_____

2. My reaction to the above incident is_____

3. My thoughts about and evaluation of my reaction are_____
   _____(core issue)

The Forgiving and Healing

A. I am grateful for the possibility of forgiving and healing

B. I take responsibility for the thoughts of (#3 above)_____
and I let go of these thoughts.

C. I release my reaction of (#2 above)_____

D. I dissolve the incident of (#1 above)_____by
turning my attention to unrelated positive thoughts, which are

_____

By completing this exercise, I have forgiven myself for my reaction to the incident above and for my thoughts about my reaction to it. Doing so forgives the person or the incident that I perceive as having been harmful to me. I am grateful and I am at peace

Signed_____

5

Obstacles To Forgiveness

A practice of any value has its obstacles and the practice of the Forgiveness Process is no exception. The most difficult obstacle you may encounter will be the selfish part of the ego that thinks it is who you are. It will jump right into the middle of your Forgiveness Process and try to take over. It will shut the gate of the soul quicker than anything else. The ego tells you that you can't forgive; that you must retaliate, get even, render to others their due, save your honor. However, the rewards of forgiving are greater than any egoistic exploits. An eye for an eye is not a good policy.

Think of the tremendous healing in the world if only a percentage of the earth's people practiced the Forgiveness Process. Bickering, infighting, war—all could be reduced or eliminated when replaced by love and forgiveness. What prevents this from happening is the irony that people's egos judge the behavior of other people's egos, instead of people accepting the sacredness of other people's humanity and respecting each other. It seems to be difficult for people to say they love each other or appreciate each other or appreciate what others do. This may be because they are caught up in the ego which takes charge and declares that everything is about me, me, me. As a result, many people will not forgive where they see nothing in it for themselves as dictated by their driving or dominating egos. So they carry grudges and walk around with long faces, trusting no one. Trust is an integral part of forgiving, but many times it is sabotaged by our self-focused ego.

There are several blocks to forgiveness. Following are some of them.

Guilt

Through guilt, we draw to ourselves much of our own suffering. Guilt is a fault-finding that heaps upon us blame when that which we say, think or do goes against old, ingrained beliefs. Guilt is like striking our chest with a dagger while chanting "through my fault" without realizing that we just keep stabbing ourselves. Therefore, we never stop bleeding and never forgive. The ego, while a good part of our guidance through life, seems to lean us toward the negative. However, it can be returned to its place and peace can be restored through non-resistive surrender and forgiveness. Nonresistance is like a flower bud allowing its petals to open; non-resistive surrender is the open blossom turning to face the sun. By application of this analogy, we allow the guilt to be exposed, which is non-resistance, and turn to the Source of love to surrender the guilt and let it be washed away, an act of non-resistive surrender. This is a self-forgiving process that eliminates guilt.

Pride and Sacrifice

There are ample issues to which we can apply the practice of forgiveness. For instance, one such issue is pride, an ever-present bane of society; not pride as in one's accomplishments, but the pride of self-infatuation and aggrandizement. Pride absorbs the lives of many people who make the mistake of thinking they are superior to others if they give of themselves, their time or their effort on another's behalf. These endeavors may be considered sacrificial. But sacrifice limits giving and, under the principle of give and receive, it also limits receiving. Healing the limitations of pride necessitates forgiving self through the Forgiveness Process.

Let's go deeper into the idea of sacrifice because the pride of it can be lodged deep in the ego. True service is not sacrificial in that you need not deny your own needs to provide the needs of another. Do not confuse this with sharing, which is of a higher nature and is not the issue here. Non-ego based service, with respect toward another, is giving both yours and the other's needs the same priority, and the service is a choice. For example, if you are motivated to jump into a cold river to rescue a drowning person, your action is not sacrificial, for your priorities and the drowning person's priorities are equal: you both want to live. One person's desire to do so is no greater than the other's. After you pull the drowning person out of the water, neither one or the other is the winner. You both are, for you both suffered equally in that you both got wet and cold and faced the risk of drowning. Neither of you is the hero, or you both are.

So where does the Forgiveness Process fit into the example of the drowning person? It applies the same as in any other incident where there is ego involvement. The incident or issue in the drowning rescue may be egotistical pride before you jump into the water. Later, your reaction to the incident of pride may be that you think you are superior, that no one else would have jumped into the cold river like you did. Your feeling about this reaction of superiority may suddenly turn to thoughts of shame and embarrassment as you realize your truth. To restore your peace in this example, give thanks, let go the shame or embarrassment and release the thought of being better than others. Then dissolve your engaging pride and any thought of it by focusing, perhaps appropriately, on humble service. Finally, enjoy the peace of knowing that all is one, that everyone is the same. The same force pumps life through you and through the person you pulled out of the water. You both are of the same Essence.

Surrender rather than sacrifice is the more spiritual and peaceful path. In surrender, you still give of yourself but, instead of seeing the act as an imposition on your time, effort or resources, you perceive the service as love toward another human being and ultimately, under the principle of oneness, as love of Self. The work called for in this instance is surrendering the act and accepting what is in the present moment. Your action then is from a higher motive, one from which you receive more than you give. When you surrender sacrifice, you lift yourself to higher levels and receive in return the peace that is God.

Surrender leads the way to forgiveness, the letting go and dissolving of the thought of whatever is to be forgiven. As we have seen, to release a hurt or an attachment, it is the thought about the reaction to the hurt or attachment that must be let go. Thought always empowers that about which we think. Once we no longer think about something, it dissipates. If we resist releasing the thought, we resist the acceptance of what is, because surrender is accepting. For instance, blaming someone for our misfortune is resistance, perhaps resistance to personal responsibility. Once the reaction to the thought of blaming is surrendered and let go, it is transcended. Then healing takes place and the blame is dissolved. This is what takes place in the Forgiveness Process.

The Negative Side of Affirmations

An affirmation is a statement that programs our mind with the hope of attracting positive spiritual conditions or material manifestations. Affirmations are power. They are the thoughts and words that create. However, beware! We may have subconscious underlying beliefs to the beliefs we choose to affirm as true. This is where "yes, but" shows up. Pay attention to this, for it can lead to difficulties and frustrations. For example, if you are healthy, there is no need for the affirmation "1 am healthy". However, if you are ill, you may state the affirmation "1 am healthy" but the actual underlying belief may shout "yes, but", a protest from deep inside you because you do not feel healthy. The underlying belief is "I am sick". If it were not so, you would not even think of saying the affirmation. Similarly, a person in need of finances may affirm a true belief of "I am rich". The actual underlying belief, however, the "yes, but" protest which appears as reality, is "I am poor".

In making affirmations, it is difficult to focus on the preferred or intended condition, the one to be affirmed, when there is a strong "yes, but" belief. This is because the actual underlying belief, which appears as reality, keeps popping up. Affirmations of the actual underlying belief - of illness for example - should be stated as a denial of the condition by stating the true belief as "even though I appear to be sick, I am healthy". At this point, you have a great opportunity to choose what belief you carry forward. Affirming health, the sick person may develop a belief in health so strong that the body responds to the stimulation and heals at the speed of surprise. There is power in affirmations, but take care in choosing the condition you affirm, carefully screening your intention. Your body listens and responds to what you say–and think!

In the affirming process, just as in trust and forgiveness, the ego may rise up and try to take charge. To illustrate, let's assume that you actually are sick. This is the 'incident' as described in the Forgiveness Process. Your reaction to being sick may be to say the affirmation "I am healthy". But unless you really believe your affirmation–and that should be your intention–your reaction to the affirmation may be "yes, but I have this hacking cough, this fever, I feel lousy, etc., etc., etc. How can I be healthy?" That is the underlying belief, and the ego reinforces it. Now you may suddenly develop thoughts of remorse or shame about your reaction, about thinking this way; or you may feel regret for doubting your power of affirmation and the power of your body to heal. To resolve this issue, give thanks for the possibility of healing and let go the thoughts of shame, doubt or remorse about your reaction to your affirmation. Then, release the reaction itself and dissolve the thought of sickness by thinking positive thoughts that are unrelated to illness. Now enter into surrender, tranquility and peace and allow healing to enter your life. (You may recognize the 7 steps of the Forgiveness Process in the above example.)

The Vacuums of Life

Practicing the Forgiveness Process creates something akin to a vacuum in your life, a void that was occupied by the surrendered and released thoughts, emotions or feelings–hatred, for example. Into this vacancy, you must consciously channel a positive replacement, like love or compassion. If you don't, you can expect one of two things to occur. One may be that the old thing you released, like the hatred, will return and continue to fester. The other may be that something will enter that you do not want, like judgement or impatience. The emotional vacuum cannot remain a vacuum. Something must fill it. With concentration, focus and effort, you can fill it with attributes you want, thus creating your life and your joy.

Your spiritual growth is not by acquiring these attributes, but by discarding, eliminating and renouncing that which covers and hides the attributes already in you. The vacuum created by practicing forgiveness allows the exposure of those attributes. By analogy, when the clouds disappear, the sun that was always there is revealed. In practicality, when your clouds–the forgiven aspects of your life–are removed, heaven, which is always in you, shows up.

To understand the creation of a vacuum in your life, it may help to visualize an example. Suppose we go to the beach and dig a hole in the sand near the water. The sand we dig out of the hole represents that which was surrendered in the Forgiveness Process. The hole represents the vacuum. If the hole is deep enough, and we do nothing, sea water will seep in and fill it. The hole fills with water because it is next to water. Similarly, a vacuum, a void, in us will be filled with whatever is next to us. If we do nothing and we are next to hate, the void will fill with hate; if we are next to God, then God-like things rush in to fill the emptiness. But if we do something, like engaging the powers of will and intention, we can stop the hate, for instance, from filling our vacuum and instead allow it to be filled with something positive that we would rather have. The nature of a vacuum is such that it cannot remain a vacuum and it draws to itself and fills itself with whatever is near and available. This is a very important point to remember in the releasing and letting go steps of the Forgiveness Process, for these are acts that create vacuums in our lives.

This process of creating vacuums goes on for a lifetime, every time we release, let go and forgive. Forgiveness propels us forward and cleanses us so that we see life not as it is, but as we are. From this, we can know ourselves to be sacred, spiritual lights that no longer conform to the world's perception of us. We now relate to the world according to our perception of our Self, free of other's opinions. We acknowledge being healed, regenerated, renewed. We are grateful and God takes our gratitude, wraps it in divine love and returns it to us as fulfillment of our intentions. Truly, angels rejoice with us.

Prelude To Chapter Six

Immortal Mind
Born into time
To manifest Eternal Being
As mankind.
                    Henry Petru

6

Healing The Obstacles—

Compassion and Love

The world hardly knows the power of a soul at peace. Peaceful compassion toward suffering, even toward the self, is an aspect of the enlightened soul. Compassion is like gently touching a baby that is crying, understanding that the baby is merely expressing its distress in the only way it knows. A non-peaceful adult may react to the baby's cry with an act that will calm the baby not for its sake, but for the adult's sake, perhaps because the adult is irritated by the crying. The adult gets irritated because the baby's cry awakens something of the adult's own pain and fear that the adult does not want to face. On the other hand, a peacefully compassionate person shows concern and simply calms the baby because the baby is crying.

Similar interactions take place among adults. Some try to comfort the distress of another so that they will not have to face their own distress. The self-discovered person, however, in a state of unattached compassion, supports the expression and the healing of another's distress. Empowered by having learned how to forgive, the soul at peace walks softly in love upon the earth.

Compassionate love, surrender and forgiveness constitute personal powers. Love there always is, but enhancing it with forgiveness allows you to express life from your Self internally - that is, by giving–and from your neighbor externally–that is, by receiving. Living these powers, you and your neighbor come together as if both of you are nibbling on the same noodle, each from opposite ends. At some point, you will come together and kiss and there will be no more noodle, nothing more to let go and forgive. Love will be the only thing left.

Compassionate awareness and compassionate love give us the power to surrender, release and let go. These are processes that change life from chaotic existence to a peaceful understanding of our place in the present moment. In that moment, we need no answers because there are no questions. If they exist, the questions are the same as the answers and they appear simultaneously.

Love your Self as your neighbor because, within the principle of Oneness, your neighbor is your Self. You are so important that life is incomplete without you. You are like a piece of a

Tiffany lampshade or a piece of a stained-glass window; if you are missing, no other piece will fit just right. Only you can fill that particular space. You, as the Essence that is God, are needed to complete existence. Not that God diminishes any by creating you, but God projected you out of Self and left an opening for you to return and only you fit that opening. Without you, there is an eternal space, an empty spot, where you belong. Loving yourself and your Self create the love out of which all things go out from you and by which all things return to you. You are magnificently wonderful, marvelously beautiful, and unavoidably important.

Because you complete creation, ultimately you do not belong in this world. You arrive, visit and depart the earth because you are of a Higher Source. You stay only for a little while, alleviating suffering by accepting it, dissolving it and letting it go through the power of forgiveness, and you do not leave until your work is done. You were given a body as the vehicle to carry you from your spiritual level at physical birth, through your existence of physical life, to your spiritual level at physical death. You, like every other human being, leave this world on time. No one dies prematurely, or past their time. To say so would be a human judgment by which we assume privilege in knowing how long a certain person was supposed to live on earth. No one leaves prematurely, whether at age 90 years, 20 years or 6 months. When you leave this planet, finished and complete, your new reality awaits you like the ocean awaits a drop of rain. You arrive on the next level fully fruited, complete and at the peak of perfection, ready to dissolve back into the Almighty Ocean.

Prelude To Chapter Seven

If you're not living on the edge,
you're taking up too much space.
                                    Anonymous
(by an old woman in a nursing home)

7

Helps To Forgiveness—

Sanctuary Practices

Author's Note: The inspiration for this chapter in particular came to me during time spent in the sanctuary of my bathroom. Because I truly consider my bathroom as being a sanctuary, I refer to these visits as sacred moments. Information in this chapter explains how to incorporate and align the acts of surrender, release and letting go with the habits and functions of physical release and cleansing. These applications empower and enhance the effectiveness of the Forgiveness Process.

Forgiveness is empowering, and surrender, a precursor to forgiving, is one of the most powerful of human acts, for it entails letting go of judgement and blame, two facets of ourselves affecting our self-image. In this context, judgements declare for ourselves what we believe others deserve, and that belief lodges within our being. Thus, judgements are criticisms of ourselves. Blame, on the other hand, is confessing that of which we accuse others. Blame and judgement bind us to pain and suffering and must be surrendered, dissolved and let go as a prerequisite to forgiving.

As an example, consider this metaphor. Suppose you tie one end of a rope to a large rock lying on the ground near a cliff, tie the other end to your foot, and shove the rock over the edge of the cliff into the valley below. You could think you have surrendered the rock to the valley, but reality comes very quickly. You can blame the rope, the rock, or whatever you feel is responsible, but the fact is that you're lying crushed in the valley at the base of the cliff through your own doing.

Metaphysically, the rock can be considered as, let's say, an event of anger and the rope as your attachment to that anger. Surrendering the rock–the anger–is a huge beginning in clearing it but you're still attached to it and you are pulled over the cliff. To free yourself, you must sever the attachment, the rope. It must be let go. Dissolving this binding hold is accomplished through forgiveness. Until this is done, the anger will persist and your attachment to it will hold fast. You will always end up crushed at the base of the cliff.

Untying or cutting the rope severs the grip of the anger, surrenders control and invites your Higher Self to take over. You develop a trust and a knowing in your heart that Universal Power knows your good. Listening to this power through intuition, the voice of your Higher Self, you can surrender the judgements and blame that compel you to push the rock of anger, or of anything else to which you are attached, over a cliff.

Surrender is a decision that shifts attitude, and attitude is a power that lets you wallow in the mud or inspires you to rise to the stars. All actions stem from attitude, for what you do is determined by the way you see life, your perception of yourself and the world around you. Peace and happiness are spawned by an attitude of loving all that is. Anything less may usher in discomfort and misery.

Sometimes, a strange attitude about self and life causes people to do strange things. For instance, people appear on TV talk shows and expose their most personal secrets, even become violent on the show, and the audience claps and cheers. It seems idiotic. Perhaps the motivation of people appearing on these shows is to gain approval and feel loved. Perhaps they receive very little approval and love from anyone else and may experience such a low level of self-esteem that they cannot even approve of themselves. Consequently, they don't care if they admit to or do strange things in front of the public. They accuse, judge and blame, but may not have the capacity to forgive and love.

Ultimately, the feeling about self and about everyone and everything originates in our inner being. The way we handle our reactions to people and situations is the way we feel about ourselves and about life in general. Whatever the situation, it is always about us, not about them or it. The way we react determines our peace or chaos, and it is based on the esteem and perception of self-worth, which operates from an inherent blueprint of well-being. If our reaction is chaos, that is, if it is a meaningless jumble, the need may be to surrender the feeling of chaos and release our reaction to the way we feel about ourselves. We can choose to believe that the chaos is normal, thereby choosing to experience misery. On the other hand, we can choose to dissolve the chaos by experiencing it and living through it, thereby achieving a new level of well-being and strength. Since chaos has no blueprint, it cannot reconstitute once it is dissolved, and well-being, which does have a blueprint, prevails. This process incorporates the elements of forgiveness as discussed in chapter four.

In the process of forgiving, we discover attributes that exist in us, and have existed in us, from the beginning. Retreating to a private place may offer some opportunities to discover these attributes and to find ways within us to honor ourselves. Have you ever noticed where you are and under what conditions you do your best thinking? What place triggers your inspiring thoughts? Where can you go to ponder in privacy these principles of attitude, self worth, surrender, forgiveness and letting go? Many such places exist. The bathroom in your home is one such place and it is a powerful place, for there you are alone and really get personal with yourself, renewing by cleansing and eliminating what no longer serves you. The shower and the commode become your tools for in-depth spiritual and emotional surrender, release and letting go. You can realize much spiritual healing in the bathroom if you hold an open attitude about the natural functions that take place there. The odors there may as well be those of released anger, hatred, jealousy, greed and other imperfections. They all stink! Additionally, washing the body in the shower helps generate ideas because showering stimulates thinking by focusing attention on the body. We think with our whole body, not with just our brain. The brain is the link to the mind, which is imbedded in the energy surrounding the body.

In some circles, surrender and letting go are practiced in a variety of rituals. One is the burning bowl ceremony. In this ceremony, what is to be let go and forgiven is written down on a piece of paper which then is burned in a container as an act of release and surrender. It can be an inspiring practice. However, in the sanctuary of the bathroom, you can ritualize a daily practice that is just as effective by saying affirmations, meditating, or praying during physical elimination, a time when the whole body is involved. A suggested simple saying may be: "I release and let go (anger) from my life, and I dispose of it as waste." The Universe loves symbolism and, as your body releases, so can your heart, mind and spirit. After this, the flush dispenses everything physical, mental and emotional and becomes as symbolic as the burning of the paper cited above. The personal empowerment of this practice can be truly astounding. The act of elimination in this practice corresponds to steps "A" through "D" in the Forgiveness Process outlined in chapter four.

The practices outlined in this chapter enhance the awareness that you are sacred of God. So, mindfully respect yourself and give gratitude for a healthy body. If you're working on releasing a specific issue, pray or affirm the release, by whatever words come to you, while the body is in elimination. As an example, I'll describe my personal practice. At the time of this writing, 1 am working on ridding my life of all negative judgements. The following is my bathroom exercise. During elimination, I make an affirmation similar to this:

"I am grateful for the possibility of healing. I release all negative judgements from my life and I let them go. I forgive myself for harboring ill thoughts about others and I dispose of these judgements as waste. Thank you, my body, for perfect functioning. I love you. I honor and respect you. Thank you, God, for this wonderful body, my beautiful home on earth. I am deeply grateful."

Let your prayer reflect your sincerity, respect, love and gratitude. If you focus on the spiritual aspects of this practice, your experience truly can be amazing and profoundly soul-stirring.

The above exercise may generate a laugh or a chuckle about such an idea. Some may even find it repulsive. But there is no mystery here and no reason to "de-sanctify" your bathroom. Creative Source, whatever that is to you and by whatever name you call it, knows what's under your clothes and how your body works and a prayer for a healthy bowel is the same as a prayer for healthy eyesight, or for any other organ or function. All are sacred, one no more than the other.

In the shower, washing the body is an act of letting go and it may be enhanced by the sound of the water and perhaps by your singing or humming. But don't wait to get into the shower to sing. You may want to start singing as soon as you enter the bathroom, for this helps create a happy place. Sing from your heart. If you like, you can just hum, but make it spiritual, whatever that is for you. If you feel good about this activity, the melody will flow.

After you have cleaned the body and before you turn off the shower, stand with a strong water spray directed to your chest and close your eyes. Be sure you stabilize yourself to prevent falling. Now hum or tone in as Iowa pitch as you can. Toning "AH" or "O" are good low vibratory sounds you might try. Feel the tones rumble deep in your throat and chest. The vibrations you experience will feel like a chest massage: the shower externally and your voice internally. If you can, imagine yourself being one with the water. Do not sing at this point; just hum or tone in a low pitch. At best, these vibrations set up a resonance in your chest and can take you to a higher emotional and spiritual state. At minimum, the exercise will give you a present moment experience. Do this for a short time—or for as long as you wish.

After your shower and toweling, I suggest this powerful exercise. Stand naked facing a mirror where you can see your face and at least your upper body. Fold your hands in front of you as in prayer and reverently bow a blessing in gratitude to yourself, honoring your body, the temple of your Being. Respectfully look at your body and tell it, in whatever words come to you, that you love it the way it is. Harbor only positive thoughts about your body. No criticism! You, as is everyone else, are of the greatest energy in the universe and, looking at yourself, you see nothing more or nothing less than you see when looking at any other human being. At this point, you may begin to experience unfamiliar emotions and feelings. Surrender to what you feel and let the sensations enable your spiritual empowerment. Release any attempt to control these feelings; let them flow freely. It may help to close your eyes at this point, for you may feel a power that is new to you. Bask in it. Let this feeling take you into higher realms. Then, when you are ready, open your eyes and look directly into them in the mirror and tell yourself–your spirit–that you love who you are. Look for as long as it feels comfortable. Bear in mind that the image in the mirror is the reflection of a being worthy of all reverence. You are sacred. Again, when you are ready, fold your hands in prayer and bow to yourself in gratitude and respect. Following this, you may want to "just be" for a moment, for you may feel a glow or a tingling in your body.

At some point, the moment will come when you know that your bathroom prayer and meditation are finished. You may experience freedom from anxiety, fear, anger and stress and feel instead peace and harmony. But be aware that negative feelings about yourself may arise during the mirror work. Know that when you truly love yourself, the faults or shortcomings you perceive might make you feel uncomfortable. It is important that you not put yourself down over these feelings, but instead, forgive yourself for whatever they cause you to feel and for how you feel about them. This calls for the practice of the Forgiveness Process.

If the mirror exercise was done with sincerity and love, you may recognize that what you see in the mirror, and all that this evokes within you, is the totality of your world suspended in the loving universe of your Self. All events and all people that enter your life after this are like meteorites entering your personal atmosphere. Some blaze in glory across your sky like sparklers, giving you warmth, good feeling and purpose. Others crash into your life and make chaos and craters. To regain serenity and harmony from this chaos, always return to the beauty of your inner and outer self–the experience with the mirror–where you can heal the craters and give gratitude for the sparklers.

Sometimes it may be difficult to determine exactly what to surrender or release. The exact issue may be elusive. However, if you are open and receptive, the bathroom practices trigger that which needs to be let go. It will show up without being forced. Once the issue surfaces, it is not to be examined, pondered upon or analyzed. Simply acknowledge it, wrap it in love and let it go through the Forgiveness Process. Once it is disposed, let that be the end of it. You may discover how heavily the burden weighed on your spirit once it is released and, to your relief, how lighthearted and emotionally free you feel after it is let go.

By now, you need no reminder that the Forgiveness Process is not easy. For help and for answers, I often go to nature. The following lesson from nature helps me understand how to do the releasing part of the Forgiveness Process. If we observe an eagle as it launches from its perch, we will find that as the eagle launches, it leans forward, spreads its wings and releases its grip on the perch just an instant before it starts flapping its wings. The eagle could flap all day but never take to the air if it did not release its hold on the perch. Applying this to the Forgiveness Process, we may figuratively flap our wings trying to get away from our problems, but we refuse to let go of our comfortable perch, to surrender, release and let go. We're anchored and attached to the comfortable feeling of perching and are afraid to change. To change, we must surrender, release and let go. Then we can soar.

If we resist surrendering and forgiving, we suffer discomfort and pain. It is not the situation, but the resistance to it, the reaction to what is in the moment, that causes the pain. The choice to resist, or not to resist, empowers us to be sad or happy, respectively. When we accept non-resistance, we choose not to resist and choose instead to open to accepting what is, happiness and joy flow to us in huge torrents. Do not shut the door to this happiness and joy, for surrender is empowering and is fueled by trust. Only through honest and authentic surrender of self, and trust in Self, can we truly live the edict "Thy will be done".

A Postscript

Thousands of years ago, Buddha stated: "Hatred does not cease by hatred at any time; hatred ceases by love. This is an unalterable law". Before we go on to the next chapter, I must offer a thought concerning hatred and anger since they are at the root of so many problems, making them high priority candidates for the Forgiveness Process. Anger is a self-image issue. It is directly related to one's personal value and belief system, and its intensity is proportional to one's level of that value and belief. An unhappy, radical mind will look for any excuse to be angry. Hatred, likewise, is a self-image issue. Both are emotions, feelings sparked by thoughts. They put the angry person in the place of the person, place or situation at which the hatred and anger are directed. If you suffer the misfortune of having hatred or anger arise in you, it may help to ask yourself: "Why am I angry at this? Why do I hate this?" As you ask the questions, notice your thoughts behind the feeling of anger or hatred, your reaction to these thoughts. To heal the hatred and anger, use the steps of the Forgiveness Process outlined in chapter four to shift your focus, your thought, from "being angry at" to "being angry because", and from "just hating it" to "hating it because". These are the thoughts behind the reaction to the emotions of anger and hatred. In this way, the hatred and anger can be released by letting go and surrendering the thoughts, which dissolve the feelings. The banishment of hatred and anger from your life will reward you with an uncommon peace. The world becomes a wonderful place once you remove these from your life.

Prelude To Chapter Eight

Moment,
Where is your grip?
Why have you slipped
From my grasp
When I'm not finished with you?
Moment,
You're the instant
Whence I've come,
Whither I go,
Where happen all things I do.
Henry Petru

8

The Present Moment—

The Only "Time" To Forgive

Since we cannot forgive in the past or in the future, but only in the present, it is appropriate and helpful to write something in this book about "time". Everything you have read in this book so far, you have read in the present moment. What you remember about what you have read is a memory of a past event—the event being the reading of this book. Understanding the present moment deepens the understanding of forgiveness. In forgiving, what you release pertains to everything that is not in the absolute present. If you think you're forgiving an incident in the present, you are not. You would have to be doing the forgiving as the incident is in the process of happening. That's hardly possible since a step in the Forgiveness Process involves experiencing a feeling about your reaction to the incident. All forgiven incidences are of the past or the future, two entities that do not exist in present reality. Therefore, when the ideas of a past and a future are let go, only the real present remains. That's where everything exists. So the question arises: where do we live? Is it in our thoughts, in our bodies, in our emotions? Our answer to that question tells us who we are in the moment, either balanced in life or dominant in some area. Nothing just happens. Life is a synchronistic progression of the awareness of what exists in the present moment. Actually, the awareness of what is about to happen is the real present, and this awareness is just a flick ahead of what is beginning to happen. It is followed by the action of the actual happening, whether physical, emotional, or mental. Put another way, the present moment is the space just ahead of the awareness of what's happening, like the shock wave off the nose of an airplane after it goes through the sound barrier. We could say that the shock wave closest to the airplane is the awareness of the present moment, and the airplane is the happening event. But what is happening right now is already in the past the very instant it happens. If you say "hello", the greeting is past as soon as it is spoken. In linear time, the present experience is the past and the immediate future is the present. A real future has no basis of reality in linear time. It can only be imagined.

This knowledge has a direct influence on our lives. When we learn to live in the moment, in the "right now", we find that what irritated or bothered us before no longer does so. The present moment has no room for boredom or monotony. Consider that a moment has no beginning or ending, and the present moment is a continuous, momentous flow. "Time", as a progression of events, does not stop. Therefore, anyone point in "time" becomes a past moment the instant it happens.

As already stated, understanding the present moment deepens understanding of forgiveness. Toward this end, envision the present moment as looking down a hallway. Beyond the wall on the left is designated as the "past", which you cannot see. Beyond the wall on the right is designated as the "future", which also you cannot see. You can see only the hallway in front of you, representing the present. Focus on and live in this present "hallway" and whatever your life is in that moment manifests in front of you. Everything exists in the hallway of the present.

Considering that the present moment of the hallway is very short in duration of "time", it collapses as the walls of the "past" and "future" close in, even squeezing the hallway of the present almost out of existence. What this means is that the present moment is infinitely narrow; "time" wise. It is of such a short time span that it has almost no duration at all. It is simply the infinite "is," lasting no time and being eternally now. It is not easy to squeeze our life into the present moment. Yet, that is where we do live; that is where forgiveness takes place. Another "hallway" example can be found in the book of Exodus in the Bible where Moses parted the Red Sea. We can draw a parallel to the analogy of the present moment hallway mentioned earlier. The walls of water can represent the "past" and the "future", as in the hallway example. When the walls of water closed in, they came crashing down on the path of now, collapsing the present moment and leaving only that which is. In this world, it is impossible to imagine that infinite present instant. Yet, in the spirit world, that's all there is.

The concept of the present moment challenges us with some strange phenomenon. For instance, it does not allow the setting of goals or making of appointments. Let's say, for example, that you make an appointment with a dentist for 2 p.m. tomorrow. Two o'clock tomorrow does not exist in reality, only in the imagination. If it exists, it does so right now, in this instant. So to arrive at 2 p.m. tomorrow, you release the sense of time and live "now" in the present, allowing the earth to rotate to the point that you and the dentist perceive as a designated point on an instrument called 2 p.m., and you show up. Time is a physical event developed by humanity and it disappears in the Infinite Instant. Even the idea of "present moment" is a measurement of time. It is difficult indeed to live on earth in the present. To do so requires erasing a sense of time and simply being.

"Time" is a thought, a relative hook; glue to which we stick. It is a reference to which we tie our lives and it becomes the cause of incalculable tension and stress. For instance, you are to meet someone at a "time" in the day indicated by two pointers on a dial, or by lit numbers in a little window. Let's call that indication 2 p.m., as in the example above. You arrive, and the other person is not there, or the person with whom you have an appointment–a doctor, let's say–is not "on time". Do you go into stress by getting angry that someone is "wasting your time"? Once again, we ask "what is time"? In the macrocosmic world, time is a measurement of the rotation of the earth on its axis, the revolution of the moon around the earth, or the revolution of the earth around the sun, among others. Can you "waste" that? So, stress can be avoided by remaining present, calm and peaceful and rescheduling your appointment, to yourself, on the spot. Here's how. Admit to yourself that you arrived early for a 2:15 appointment. The same applies if the doctor is late. In that case, you simply have arrived early. This way you remain in the present moment as much as is possible and avoid stressful and tense feelings. Your body and spirit respond to the peace and tranquility as you wait, mindful that there is only "this moment". Then, you can calmly greet the other person with a smile when he/she shows up at 2:10, for instance, or when your name is called at 2:05 for your self-rescheduled 2:15 appointment. You can even express gratitude that everything is happening "ahead of schedule". Will you miss any following commitment by doing this? When you believe in and trust synchronicity, you will have sufficient "time" to get to your next appointment or to the next place for you to be. But if you challenge this process just to put it to the test, it will not work. But if you believe it and flow with it, "time" will slow down for you. Trust it! Believe it! Live it! Live with what is before you and do not be concerned with what's ahead. That is living in the present.

Time is only a reference point. Consider this example. Suppose you lived on a planet in our solar system that we'll name "Blue". Suppose Blue is locked to the sun the way the earth's moon is locked to the earth, that is, nonrotating so that the same area always faces the sun. Since there is no rotation of planet Blue, what would your experience of "time" be? Supposed you had no instruments to calculate or measure anything, including Blue's orbit around the sun. Would you experience "time"? At whatever place you lived on Blue, life would always be in the present, always the same. The sun would always be in the same place in the sky, or there would be continuous darkness if you lived on the side opposite the sun. There would be no morning, evening, midnight, noon—it would always be the same on the place where you lived. You could not plan for tomorrow or next year because these time measurements would not exist. You would eat when you got hungry, not by the clock because there would be no clock. Your body would attain a natural rhythm of its own. The only hint of "time" may be evident in your body. You may notice hair loss or wrinkles, but would these really be measurements of "time"? You would simply be, and when the instant came that your body was to cease functioning, it would simply die—not old, not young, just finished.

On earth, we actually live in the "past" and call it "the present". All that we see has already happened because the instant that we think of as "now" immediately becomes the past. The present moment is such a fleeting, thin slice of what we perceive as reality that it becomes unreal. In practical terms, the present moment time–does not exist and is, therefore, an illusion. This may explain why change is so difficult because what we try to change is actually the immediate past, and the past is already recorded and cannot be changed. So we have to deal with a sliver of present reality, and all that our life is must happen and be lived in that infinitesimal moment.

In that infinitesimal moment–the true present moment reality–the beginning and the end are the same. Living as much as possible in that moment frees us from waiting and from impatience, and allows us to be spontaneous. Spontaneity is a sweetness of life and it can only take place in the present. Ponder the following verse. I wrote it in a moment of inspiration while watching a butterfly.

> Were that life be as the insect
> Which neither ponders nor plans,
> Yet has beauty to show and joy to give,
> And is present right now
> Simply because it has life to live.

Thomas Troward, in his book "The Creative Process In The Individual", states: *"If we accept the philosophical conclusion that time has no substantive existence, then all that remains is states of consciousness"* (Italics mine). From this, we can interpret that time does not exist, but is only a concept and the present moment only a state of consciousness. We create time when we relate one event to another. In the present moment, every event is "at once". Therefore, no relationship of events can take place. We are at peace now. But we can be very miserable when we use the present moment as a pathway to an illusory future. In the present moment, we may possibly come to know that we arrive before we depart because we are here, and there, right now. The past is done. It is finished. Nothing there can change. The future can only be imagined and visualized even though it can be anticipated with joy or apprehension. Present reality is right where we are this instant. Some things in this instant we can influence–by what we say, for example. Others we cannot–the weather, for instance. But our perception of who we are, who we are not and how we react to what is around us in the moment is the only reality there is for us. Everything else is either past or future and does not exist in reality. But when we don't know who we are, we are everything because, at that point, we are in the present moment where everything exists, including us.

As discussed at the end of chapter six, we may question why people die at what we perceive as all ages: some young, some old and some in between. Perhaps the reason is that the very life essence of us–call it our soul or our spirit–does not comprehend time since it exists in the ever-present ethereal realm. When it has completed that which it came to do in this world, it leaves the body and goes home, perhaps not even knowing how much "time" it spent in a body on earth. The soul, being of God, knows only the infinite present.

The present moment and eternity are the same instant. Mentally, we can go to the future and to the past. But physically, we can live only in this moment right now. When this moment is finished–if such a thing is possible–we live in the next moment, in a continuous slide of moments. Even eternity is one moment at a time but, since there is no time in eternity, there is no moment and eternity is an ever present now. From this we can see that our lifetime in a body is only a flash upon the earth, a flicker of existence. Hence, if there is anything to be done, it is expedient to do it now, and this applies to forgiving. Procrastination belies a belief in an illusory future, one that does not exist. Therefore, forgive everything immediately!

In linear "time", our bodies have a beginning and an end. Our thoughts do too. As an example, think of mud. Now, think of bananas. Now, think of mountains. These are separate thoughts. Each starts and ends. Between thoughts, there is an infinitesimal, tiny blank space. In that space between thoughts–the moment of the silent now–all potential and all possibilities exist because that silent moment is eternity, and eternity contains all that is. If we learn to peer into that space, we will find there the eternity of peace, harmony, love and beauty.

We will find God. Then we can find Heaven wherever we are. As we grow spiritually, we can learn to lengthen that space between thoughts, thereby living in Heaven on Earth.

9

The Rewards Of Forgiveness

The fruits of forgiveness are the empowerments of peace, happiness and joy. Joy and happiness may seem to be the same emotion, but there is some distinction between them. Joy is defined as a very glad feeling, great pleasure or delight. Happiness, on the other hand, is defined as a cause of a feeling of great pleasure or delight. So, joy is a feeling; happiness is something that causes the feeling. But both are neutral until we react to something that gives us a good feeling (joy) or until we accept something (happiness) that causes joy.

To illustrate, consider the following simple personal story. I grew up on a farm in Texas. Sometimes on a lazy afternoon, my brother and I would lie down on the ground face up and watch the clouds drift overhead. We would watch them roll and churn and merge. Some, carried by the wind, seemed just to drift. We would try to find shapes that resembled things we knew. Where we lay on the ground, there was happiness caused by the clouds, and that happiness moved us into joy.

While reading the foregoing story about the clouds, did you get a picture of a tranquil and peaceful scene? I urge you to seek this kind of happiness and catch this kind of joy in whatever gives you pleasure. Perhaps occasionally, you can look up at the clouds. This simple act will temporarily take your mind off earthly cares as you shift your attention up into the sky. Marvel and be inspired by the variety of shapes and the beauty of forms. A colorful sunset or sunrise especially can be inspiring and can mentally "take you out of this world". These moments cost nothing but can be very rich in happiness and joy. It is difficult to hold on to animosity or anger while in this state, and it is an excellent time to practice forgiveness or to enjoy the benefits of it.

How do you react to this statement: the world is a happy place. One reaction might be "oh, it certainly is". When life has meaning and we feel we have a reason and purpose for living, then we become aware of the unconditional joy and happiness available within our own selves. In the Forgiveness Process, we learned that feelings are the result of our own reactions to the events in our lives. Some reactions are happy and joyous, some are not. The Forgiveness Process can help us make happy and joyous those that are not.

The feelings of happiness and joy are more than the absence of pain and suffering. We do not have to chase happiness to the point of un-happiness or misery. Turning joy into a job may be a constant search for new experiences to stim-ulate feelings we interpret as happiness and joy. The pursuit of happiness is one of our freedoms. But there is as much joy and happiness in si-lence, stillness and solemnity as there is in any activity. Sitting in contemplative silence can bring a great awareness of the joy within. Con-templating a sunset, for instance, can give you a sense of freedom as big as the sky. This kind of freedom gives birth to joy. Life does not have to be boring. One does not even have to smile or laugh to be happy, to experience joy, or to be at peace. These feelings, the rewards of forgiving, are generated within the self. There is a solid, deep internal joy available to those who live for-giveness. Joy may be nothing more than the ex-perience of forgiving ourselves our reactions to our own feelings about events that enter our lives, as stated in the Forgiveness Process.

Picture a glass that represents the vessel of your joy, happiness and peace. This is your for-giveness container. During times when you think that life is not fair, you may wait for–and expect–someone to come along with a big pitch-er of joy and fill your forgiveness glass. When you discover and believe that you are the only one who can fill it, you will realize that, to expe-rience true joy, happiness and peace, your glass can be filled only from the pitcher inside you. You must fill your own forgiveness glass. Then, through the higher awareness of your holo-graphic IS-ness, your oneness with all, the blissful attributes of happiness, joy and peace are reflected in everyone else. Therein lay the joy and the peace that is beyond understanding.

We often equate happiness and joy with physical sensations and emotional highs. These body-centered joys do not express the true joy of spirit. When we shift perspective from body-centered to spirit-centered, the distinction becomes clear. In spirit-centered joy, we elevate to a higher state within and we experience the Essence of joy that is God. This Essence is on us like a glimmering, silvery sheen making us glow with the light of Eternal Bliss, rather than just reflecting Eternal light.

You can enter into a meditation to experience this depth of joy. One that I like is the following. (I'll write it in the first person since that's the way I do it.) After getting myself comfortable, I close my eyes and enter a calm, centered state. Soon I see before me a dazzlingly brilliant light, and I reflect it as the moon reflects the light of the sun. As I move closer, the light intensifies but I continue to look at it. Suddenly, the glowing aura around the brilliance ignites me and I move into the light, merging with it until I am totally immersed and absorbed. A feeling of an infinitely deep calm and peace settles in, and I experience happiness that is joy unto itself. There is a feeling of freedom in which I feel that I will never again have to experience the darkness of festering problems, hurts, rejections, fears and hates. At this point, I am in the realization that I am in God, the Essence of Joy Itself. Through the intimacy of Oneness, I realize that I am beyond the duality of "God and I", of separation. Instead, I am imprinted with the awareness that God, I, am One, and the dazzlingly brilliant light is who I am. I have found True Joy! True peace! Perhaps I have touched the fringe of Eternity and felt God.

It may take a few moments to return from a meditation such as this. In achieving an inner vision of this depth and an internal perception of this magnitude, we become non- judgmental; that is, our vision of the world is not one of good and not so good. Rather, we see only that everything simply IS. We do not judge it to be one way or the other. In this state of awareness, we observe a violent event or a loving act in the same way, knowing that that's what is, and that's all that is.

This observation may seem to connote apathy or non-caring, but on a higher level, in a higher state, we understand that truly, life simply IS. There is nothing more to forgive. Joy simply is and it is in everyone. One person cannot be happy without this happiness affecting everyone else in some way, no matter how minor. A pebble dropped into a pond affects the whole pond, regardless of how large the pond is. Life is holographic. What happens in one happens in all others. All people are embodiments of each other, and this constitutes oneness. In this oneness, the joy of others is our joy, and our happiness is their happiness. There really is no separation or duality and, if there are "others", they are "us". In this attitude, forgiveness becomes universal. So does love.

Epilogue

Individual practice of the Forgiveness Process may require help, and help is available through alternative healing practices. While there are many, I favor the healing energies of Reiki and of a practice called Emotional Freedom Techniques (EFT). These practices tap into the energy of the body's life force and awaken or strengthen the power of the body, mind and spirit to heal its self.

Reiki, an ancient hands-on healing technique, strengthens the body and refreshes the spirit through the body's energy centers, the chakra system. Receiving Reiki during times of practicing the Forgiveness Process can stir emotions and draw forth clarity, insight, resolve and focus. These aspects are important during the Forgiveness Process.

Emotional Freedom Techniques (EFT) tap into the body's energy meridians. Tapping on some points of these meridians, while making statements and saying affirmations, awakens the emotions, re-educates the body's energies and brings about the fulfillment of an intention. The intention can be forgiveness.

As with any difficult task, the Forgiveness Process does not have to be attempted alone. Someone or some method is always available as a resource for you. Reiki and EFT are two of these helps.

About The Author

Henry has lived in Austin, Texas, since 1977. In the 1990s, he became a Reiki Master and later a practitioner of Emotional Freedom Techniques (EFT). He has been active in The Healing Ministry in his church since 1993.

Henry was the caregiver for his wife during her last years on earth. Following her passing in the year 2000, he sought relief from grief and anger through traditional forgiveness, but these methods did not bring peace. Drawing on his experiences with death and life, his 4-plus years in a Catholic seminary, and much study, he learned what forgiveness really is: who gives it, who gets it, and how it is done. These findings are presented in this book.

Some Books That Inspire Me

References and Recommended Readings

The New Revised Standard Version Bible. Augsburg Fortress, Minneapolis

The Isaiah Effect, Gregg Braden. Three Rivers Press, 2000

The Bhagavad Gita, A New Translation, Stephen MitchelL Three Rivers Press, 2000

The Twelve Powers Of Man, Charles Fillmore. Unity Books, Unity Village, Mo

Overcoming Senior Moments, Vanishing Thoughts - Causes and Remedies; Frances Meiser, M.Ed. and Nina Anderson. New Century Publishing, 2000

Power vs Force, David R. Hawkins, M.D.,Ph.D. Hay House, Inc., 2000

Practicing The Power Of Now, Eckhart Tolle. New World Library, 2001

The Field, Lynne McTaggart. (Quill) Harper Collins Publishers, 2002

The Creative Process In The Individual, Thomas Troward. De Vorss Publications, 1991

The Power of Intention, Wayne W. Dyer, Ph.D., Hay House, 2004

A Course In Miracles, Foundation for Inner Peace, 1976

The Divine Matrix, Gregg Braden, Hay House, Inc., 2007

99625499R00065

Made in the USA
Columbia, SC
11 July 2018